How To Win At
AIR HOCKEY

(FOR LOSERS)

Lard Cake Productions

STOP.....BEING.....A.....LOSER.

STOP....

BEING.....

A.....

LOSER.

STOP.....

BEING.....

A....

LOSER.

LOSER.

STOP.....

BEING.....

A.....

LOSER.

STOP.....

BEING.....

A.....

LOSER.

STOP.....

BEING.....

A.....

LOSER.

STOP.....

BEING.....

A.....

LOSER.

STOP.....

BEING.....

A.....

LOSER.

STOP.....

BEING.....

A.....

LOSER.

STOP.....

BEING.....

A.....

LOSER.

STOP.....

BEING.....

A.....

LOSER.

STOP.....

BEING.....

A.....

LOSER.

STOP.....

BEING.....

A.....

LOSER.

STOP.....

BEING.....

A.....

LOSER.

STOP.....

BEING.....

A.....

LOSER.

STOP.....

BEING.....

A.....

LOSER.

STOP.....

BEING.....

A.....

LOSER.

STOP.....

BEING.....

A.....

LOSER.

STOP.....

BEING.....

A.....

LOSER.

STOP.....

BEING.....

A.....

LOSER.

STOP.....

BEING.....

A.....

LOSER.

STOP.....

BEING.....

A.....

LOSER.

STOP.....

BEING.....

A.....

LOSER.

STOP.....

BEING.....

A.....

LOSER.

STOP.....

BEING.....

A.....

LOSER.

STOP.....

BEING.....

A.....

LOSER.

STOP.....

BEING.....

A....

LOSER.

STOP.....

BEING.....

A....

LOSER.

STOP.....

BEING.....

A....

LOSER.

STOP.....

BEING.....

A....

LOSER.

STOP.....

BEING.....

A....

LOSER.

STOP.....

BEING.....

A....

LOSER.

STOP.....

BEING.....

A....

LOSER.

STOP.....

BEING.....

A....

LOSER.

STOP.....

BEING.....

A....

LOSER.

NOW
YOU
ARE
READY.

GO
WIN!